The Wife
A Philosophical Drama in 3 Acts

Rajeshwar Prasad

TSL Drama

First published in Great Britain in 2021
By TSL Publications, Rickmansworth

Copyright © 2021 Rajeshwar Prasad

ISBN / 978-1-914245-37-4

Dedication

All those who believed in the wedd'ng bonds
But they have been deceiv'd by One or Some –
And who have lost their lives in mirages' hands –
And the rest is woes and sorrows to them.

Characters (in order of appearance)

CARTER   28 years old, company manager, not wearing black

HELENA   25 years old, CARTER's wife, wearing red

WESTON   60 years old, retired doctor

ROBERT   35 years old, stranger wearing black

Scenario

A very large and well-decorated wildlife hotel spread in hectares of land where several people stay daily. The hotel is famous for honeymooners. It is a light and pleasant cold day in November. There are some empty benches with a few staff and guests walking around. A tea and coffee stall. A shop of general items. People wandering hither and thither. Some guests are reading newspapers. Some are watching the television screen.

WESTON is sitting on a bamboo bench near the reception desk of the Wildlife Hotel. He is smoking a cigarette and reading a newspaper. CARTER joins him. They are quite unknown to one another. CARTER is on honeymoon with his newly married wife, HELENA. CARTER and WESTON begin to talk.

After some time, HELENA comes in search of CARTER and joins them having coffee.

In the meantime, ROBERT arrives looking for his wife HELENA.

WESTON says HELENA is CARTER's wife. When HELENA says nothing, CARTER challenges ROBERT to a fight, which ROBERT accepts. Both men die.

Approximate Running Time

50 minutes

Act 1

WESTON is sitting on a bamboo bench near the reception desk of the Wildlife Hotel. He is smoking a cigarette and reading a newspaper. CARTER approaches.

CARTER: [*Stands in front of WESTON. Smoking cigarette*] Hello uncle, what is today's headline?

WESTON: [*Very gently. Giving the newspaper to CARTER*] Please sit here and see it.

CARTER: What's in it, uncle?

WESTON: You'll be surprised.

CARTER: What?

WESTON: See and read the article on page five.

CARTER: [*Reads*] A detailed survey by the ministry of social culture?

WESTON: [*Amazed*] Yes. A wonder!

CARTER: This is a factual record of our social condition.

WESTON: [*Pause*] Think a little. Fifty per cent of married people in our country get divorced.

CARTER: Really, a piece of unique research by the ministry.

WESTON: [*Seriously*] But if it continues, what will be the state of our society?

CARTER: No doubt, this shows our social tie is breaking fast. Divorce is like a social cancer.

WESTON: This is not only a matter of tie, rather also of the hollowness of mankind.

CARTER: Not for all but for those who don't wish to maintain the purity of the social institution of marriage.

WESTON: This is not a simple matter! Look around! The whole society is rotten. Man is bleeding. There are tears and tears all around us.

CARTER: [*Amazed*] What?

WESTON: There are millions of cases in the courts which are breaking the well-established systems introduced for our welfare.

CARTER: What do you mean?

WESTON: [*Confidently*] I mean to say that man is hollow. The world is hollow. The world is merciless, joyless and loveless. God doesn't exist in this cosmos.

CARTER: [*Pause*] You are saying what you see in this newspaper but it is not everything.

WESTON: Think carefully, if this rate of divorce continues to increase, what will be the condition of our society? The world will become hell.

CARTER: This is a cycle of the world which we all follow.

WESTON: How will the world continue?

CARTER: As it does!

WESTON: In this manner?

CARTER: As it goes.

WESTON: Is this a manner?

CARTER: The world is multi-mannered. We can't compel anyone to do as we do. All are free.

WESTON: [*Long pause*] Life?

CARTER: The very life as is now, and as it was in the past, and will be in the future.

WESTON: Life is one hundred per cent a lie – really, a tale full of woes and sorrows.

CARTER: No.

WESTON: What?

CARTER: [*Pause*] It seems you are feeling hopeless.

WESTON: No, I'm not hopeless. I have seen ups and downs and know its truth.

CARTER: I think and have listened to people say that in old age man loses hope.

WESTON: No.

CARTER: But I feel …

WESTON: You are quite wrong.

CARTER: How?

WESTON: I also used to listen and feel as you feel now. But my dreams were continuously shattered one by one and now it seems that my own life is a burden to me. Though I live like others, I am happy like others. But not because I think that life is happy, rather I think I have to pass the rest part of life like others.

CARTER: Are you here for some time?

WESTON: Yes. I've been here for the past three days.

CARTER: Okay. A very good thing, uncle! It's really good that you enjoy your old age here in the lap of natural romance!

WESTON: I've come here each year for the last thirty years. I spent my honeymoon here too. So, this place is a most memorable place for me.

CARTER: [*Pause*] Is your wife dead?

WESTON: No!

CARTER: Why have you not come with her?

WESTON: [*Shows her photograph*] She's here.

CARTER: Where is she?

WESTON: In the cabin, number fifty-five.

CARTER: Yes … yes. Just opposite mine.

WESTON: In which cabin you are?

CARTER: Number twenty-seven.

WESTON:	Ah, I have seen you enter the cabin with a smart young lady.
CARTER:	When?
WESTON:	At noon.
CARTER:	I was not there at noon.
WESTON:	But I saw a smart lady in a red outfit with a handsome man in black enter the same cabin. He looked like you.
CARTER:	I never wear black clothes.
WESTON:	But I have seen a man in black very very close to your wife.
CARTER:	[*Pause*] It may be an illusion?
WESTON:	No! I'm sure!
CARTER:	[*Long pause*] Let it go.
WESTON:	Okay. I have been passing time with my old wife on the opposite side cabin.
CARTER:	Yes, I have also seen you enter your cabin with a lady who looks about fifty-five, with light wrinkles and black spots on her face. Her garments were red.
WESTON:	[*Shows a photograph of honeymoon days*] Yes, yes. She is my wife. She was very charming in her youth. But her beauty sank as ice melts in summer. Now she seems as a drum to be beaten for sounds – a woman to be carried on shoulders in the name of values and virtues which are also meaningless, like all other things.
CARTER:	[*Looks at the photograph*] I understand the reason behind your hopelessness.
WESTON:	You misunderstand.
CARTER:	What?
WESTON:	You don't understand the real issue.
CARTER:	I understand everything.
WESTON:	I also felt the very thing which you feel now. But now all that seems childish. All those dreams have been shattered. I am shamed when I recall them.

CARTER:	I have seen such men. I have met such men and found they suffer for their own reasons and try to establish a faith that the world is hollow.
WESTON:	You are quite wrong.
CARTER:	I'm right. You are wrong.
WESTON:	You have fallen into the dilemma and in this very state you will die like all others.
CARTER:	The world is full of pleasure and beauty.
WESTON:	I'm sure! You live in a state of dreams – you live in a world of expectations.
CARTER:	I live in the real world.
WESTON:	No.
CARTER:	Why?
WESTON:	[*Very seriously*] Be sure, one day you will know the world as it really is. The world of thorns! The world is a cheater which compels all of us to be cheated by its formula of loss and gain – the formula of tragi-comedy. I see there is only one sound in the earth, that is loss.
CARTER:	I used to enjoy my life as a child and always feel that the world is the heaven of heavens.
WESTON:	[*Laughs*] Ha ... ha!
CARTER:	How?
WESTON:	The pleasure which you feel now, is just like bubbles. Very attractive! Erupts without any notice! Know this tone!
CARTER:	No. This is not fact.
WESTON:	[*Firmly*] This is the only fact! I'm sure!
CARTER:	[*Pause*] Are you pessimistic?
WESTON:	[*Firmly*] Optimistic!
CARTER:	Then, why do you think all this?
WESTON:	Naturally.

CARTER: Naturally, I think I'm surrounded with joys and the warmth of blessings.

WESTON: All are meaningless. Let the time come.

CARTER: [*Pause*] Do you have children?

WESTON: [*Angrily*] Don't get personal.

CARTER: Sorry. My intention is not to hurt you but rather to know something about you which I didn't know.

WESTON: Okay. I have two children.

CARTER: Male or female?

WESTON: [*Sadly*] Both female.

CARTER: Oh! You lack heirs.

WESTON: No matter.

CARTER: Okay.

WESTON: All is the same.

CARTER: How old are they now?

WESTON: Each one is a mother of two children.

CARTER: [*Pause*] Aha! You are a grandfather. Oh! You have no male issue. Now no chance for this.

WESTON: Of course! No. But I'm satisfied.

CARTER: [*Pause*] I do understand. But ...

WESTON: What?

CARTER: You are dissatisfied with your life. So, you despair.

WESTON: No.

CARTER: This is the main reason for your despair.

WESTON: It's natural. We all embrace it from birth.

CARTER: But it's unnatural for me. I always feel a high current of joy surrounding me.

WESTON: One day, you will yourself wash away this high current of joy and everything will be absurd.

CARTER: I'm sure. The sense of despair will remain far from me.

WESTON: Time will tell.

CARTER: Okay, uncle.

WESTON: [*Gives a card*] Take my address. And contact me if you wish.

CARTER: [*Takes the card*] Thanks, great uncle.

WESTON: Alright!

CARTER: What is your profession, uncle?

WESTON: I'm a pensioner.

CARTER: A pensioner?

WESTON: Yes.

CARTER: Who pays your pension?

WESTON: Government.

CARTER: Which government?

WESTON: The government of Darkland.

CARTER: How much do you get per month?

WESTON: Enough. More than you think.

CARTER: That's very handsome.

WESTON: Anyhow, I manage.

CARTER: Anyhow?

WESTON: Yes.

CARTER: How much do you spend?

WESTON: Very much.

CARTER: Very much?

WESTON: Yes. Before, I got double and spent more. But now I pass my life on half. So, sometimes my economic condition is 'icy'.

CARTER: Why do you not control your expenditure?

WESTON: I try, but in vain.

CARTER: You get a handsome pension. But you are dissatisfied.

WESTON: No ... no! I am satisfied like all others.

CARTER: But your emotion shows that you are dissatisfied.

WESTON: No, I'm satisfied as I have no option. None has any option except to suffer.

CARTER: [*Long pause*] Okay.

WESTON: I get a pension and it sinks as the moon on the second day of the bright side. Although I try to see.

CARTER: A unique person!

WESTON: I lock some away. But I fail to keep it and it all goes in vain.

CARTER: You should do a finance management course. It will be very beneficial for you. I've done one. So, I'm very happy.

WESTON: I've also done one. But in spite of all this the amount of pension sinks. As my age is passing fast, in the same way my expenditure passes fast.

CARTER: It seems your wife is more expensive than you.

WESTON: No, she never goes shopping. Only I go and purchase items for her use. She is satisfied with my likes and dislikes and says there is no option except to like whatever I do for her.

CARTER: It's a very good thing that your wife likes whatever you do. You are so fortunate.

WESTON: No matter to be fortunate or misfortunate.

CARTER: Why?

WESTON: None is fortunate in this cosmos – nothing is meaningful. Know it!

CARTER: [*Long pause*] I get the feeling your health is very sound.

WESTON: I was a doctor and used to maintain good health. Sometimes, I thought not to be old. But I became old. Now my body is a storehouse for diseases like dyslipidemia, Alzheimer, Parkinsons, dementia, diabetes, poor eyesight, indigestion etc. [*Shows medication*] I take ten different medications daily.

CARTER:	Ten?
WESTON:	Yes.
CARTER:	Oh!
WESTON:	I can't live without them.
CARTER:	You should stop your medicines.
WESTON:	I have tried hard, but in vain.
CARTER:	You are a retired doctor. Are you not able to treat yourself?
WESTON:	In fact, not able! You are right.
CARTER:	So how did you treat your patients ?
WESTON:	None had been treated fully. If one disease was cured, another was created automatically. In this way, the whole service passed.
CARTER:	Where did you practice?
WESTON:	I practised in the New Life Hospital.
CARTER:	Yes … yes. I recognise you.
WESTON:	How?
CARTER:	Once, I was also under your care when I suffered from fever. My father had taken me to your hospital.
WESTON:	It may be.
CARTER:	I am right. I recognised you.
WESTON:	Absolutely right. All recognise me. Now some say that I have grown old and will die within some years. Some feel that I am dead already.
CARTER:	Different men and different attitudes.
WESTON:	In fact.
CARTER:	[*Pause*] A wonder! You are a doctor, but you can't cure yourself.
WESTON:	None cures anyone. The world is a disease because we live in others' homes where we have to depend on others. None cares for us properly. So, we suffer.

[Long pause]

CARTER: Do your daughters and grandchildren look after you?

WESTON: They do but after some time I feel to be cheated – to be lost in Wasteland.

CARTER: How?

WESTON: They say they love me – they respect me – they will serve me in old age – they will not let me suffer – they will not let me embrace the sense of isolation and alienation. But ...

CARTER: What?

WESTON: *[Pause]* But.

CARTER: What do you mean to say?

WESTON: *[Long pause]* I can't say.

CARTER: Do they look after you well?

WESTON: Yes. Yes. They give me food in time. They take each and every care for me.

CARTER: Very good.

WESTON: They like to eat junk food and I also like to have some. But I am unable to digest all this. So, I avoid it.

CARTER: You do well. You should take what suits you best.

WESTON: I wish to take what tastes best.

CARTER: It's is harmful for you at your age.

WESTON: Right. So, I avoid it all.

CARTER: You are very lucky. It is a wonder that your family cares for you and are very responsible.

WESTON: *[Feeling drowsy]* Yes, I also feel all this.

[Long pause]

CARTER: *[Looks at him]* Sorry, uncle. Are you feeling tired? I am going.

WESTON: No ... no. Sit here. No problem.

CARTER: *[Pause]* Uncle, they are very good. So, don't worry.

WESTON: Yes, they say they will die for me. They say they love
           me – they say they respect me. But I am alone. So, the
           sense of fear always overwhelms me and my wife too.
           Sometimes, I dream that I am in the grave. Sometimes,
           I dream that they all have taken me to an animal farm
           and I am sleeping on dung and other wastes.

CARTER: [*Surprised*] Oh! All this?

WESTON: Yes.

CARTER: [*Pause*] Don't worry. Dreams can never be true.

WESTON: What if they do?

CARTER: [*Long pause*] But ...

WESTON: Sometimes, my wife also says that her body is a burden
           to her. How will she serve me? She also has the same
           type of dreams.

CARTER: But ...

WESTON: There is another fact. Our younger daughter likes her
           more than me. So, it seems that she will die happily
           and I will die in woes and tears.

CARTER: No ... no.

WESTON: Why not?

CARTER: They seem very obedient and responsible.

WESTON: They are not obedient. None is obedient. They always
           enquire into my bank accounts and finances.

CARTER: [*Surprised*] Do they?

WESTON: Yes ... yes.

CARTER: Very wrong!

WESTON: This is not all. My grandson asks if there is any secret
           bank account in my name.

CARTER: Very wrong!

WESTON: That's not all. When I am away from home the locks of
           my boxes and cupboards are broken. Cash is taken out
           and stolen.

CARTER:	[*Surprised*] Oh! Oh! All this?
WESTON:	Yes ... yes.
CARTER:	Do you ask them?
WESTON:	Yes.
CARTER:	What do they say?
WESTON:	They say they don't know.
CARTER:	It seems the world is very dangerous.
WESTON:	Right. The world is a volcano.
CARTER:	If your own family members do all this, it's bad. They should not do so.
WESTON:	But they do.
CARTER:	They will repent in the future. God will curse them.
WESTON:	Now I am dependent on them in this old age. They will not repent. I will repent and die. My wife also does not take interest in such matters and says to let it go. After a few days we calm down and they show their love and respect towards me. So, I forget the past. Then it starts again .
CARTER:	I also don't like the sound of this.
WESTON:	None does. But now I am compelled to bear all this happily in old age. My old age has become a tattered coat on a stick.
CARTER:	[*Pause*] Try to avoid all this. Let it go. God will give you justice.
WESTON:	[*Long pause*] Once, I asked who will die with me. None responded. They asked me how much property I will give to them.
CARTER:	What?
WESTON:	How much property I will give to them.
CARTER:	What? What?
WESTON:	They are hungry for my property.
CARTER:	Property hunger?

WESTON:	Yes.
CARTER:	Greed number one!
WESTON:	They are hollow. They are killers.
CARTER:	Oh! I do understand your agonies in this age and reasons behind all this.
WESTON:	[*Long pause*] None will go to the graveyard with me.
CARTER:	What do you mean to say?
WESTON:	None is ready to die with me.
CARTER:	You are wrong there.
WESTON:	How?
CARTER:	It is unnatural. None dies with anyone.
WESTON:	I know all this. But they say to do all this, so I ask them. I don't want to see them dead. I ask them only. My motive is only to test them.
CARTER:	Your condition is unique.
WESTON:	You can understand the world and its people.
CARTER:	[*Long pause*] Whatsoever! But I am happy. My parents are in service and fine in health and property. I care for them and they love me. My wife also loves me. She is my breath.
WESTON:	You live in the world of dreams. This is Deathland.
CARTER:	How?
WESTON:	Now you will not know. None knows till he is compelled to know. My condition was the same. I earned and gave all that to them. But they are unjust and remain in my company only to gain my property as fully as they can.
CARTER:	They are legally entitled to take all this. So, what is wrong?
WESTON:	[*Long pause*] You should remain happy. I am happy … but not because I'm in this situation … but because I am compelled to accept this very state of said-happiness.

CARTER:	I say to compromise. I say avoid something. They will also grow old. They will reap the fruits of their own deeds.
WESTON:	Whether they get them or not, but what will be got by me after my death?
CARTER:	This is the law of the world which we all embrace.
WESTON:	I know.
CARTER:	I suggest avoiding some things.
WESTON:	Not some thing, rather all things I avoid.
CARTER:	[*Pause*] They should understand your feelings. One day, each one will have to embrace old age.
WESTON:	[*Long pause*] Sometimes, I feel I am alone in this world.
CARTER:	But ...
WESTON:	What?
CARTER:	Man should always control his passions and emotions.
WESTON:	All control. All fail and all dwell in Deathland.
CARTER:	It may be ... but ...
WESTON:	All may be but there is no love. There is no God. There is no joy.
CARTER:	Believe God. He will award joy to you according to your deeds.
WESTON:	Yes, I do know and hear. I worship our Maker, but only for satisfaction expecting something good. But all go in vain.
CARTER:	Uncle, believe. God is ever just.
WESTON:	The godless world. The loveless world. The world of expectations. The world of violence. The world of tears and blood. No more than all this!
CARTER:	None should challenge the existence of God.
WESTON:	I'm sure. There is nothing in its name. God doesn't exist in this cosmos.
CARTER:	You don't know the world and its reality.

WESTON: You don't know.

CARTER: [*Loud*] I know.

WESTON: [*Loud*] I know.

CARTER: I don't like to talk unnecessarily. I don't like to discuss futile topics.

WESTON: Man should discuss everything he can.

CARTER: God is not a subject for discussion.

WESTON: This is the best and the greatest subject.

CARTER: I firmly believe Him and am happy. He gives us everything. Even a leaf can't move without His mercy.

WESTON: I do think. But now I find that God is a myth to narrate verbally from generation to generation – a hanger to hang man in darkness.

CARTER: I've felt His power and empire. He is supreme. None can challenge Him. I worship Him and receive his fruit. Everything goes well I think. I manage everything as I think. Nothing bad happens to me or to members of my family. My family members also do all this. My grandparents used to suggest not losing faith in Him as He is supreme. He is beyond question. Questioning His existence is a great sin.

WESTON: [*Laughs*] Ha ... ha ... ha! You are a fool. You don't know.

CARTER: What?

WESTON: Nothing.

CARTER: What?

WESTON: What is sin? What is virtue?

CARTER: All know. All do according to its concept.

WESTON: What is obtained by man doing all this? All one gets is only woes, loss, and death.

CARTER: All this is part of life. So, we should ignore it and try to keep away from it by doing virtuous deeds.

WESTON: Virtuous works can't enable anyone to be free from the reign of Death ... to be free from the futility of life.

CARTER: I know. But it's natural.

WESTON: Life is for death naturally. But death is for life?

CARTER: All this is meaningless. We should not think about all this. It is natural and none can ignore it. So, our approach should be always positive.

WESTON: Positive approaches can't stop death.

CARTER: Without death, there is no life.

WESTON: Quite wrong.

CARTER: No.

WESTON: Yes.

CARTER: How?

WESTON: Do you know the future? Have you seen the next world? Do you know your past? Do you know your length of stay here?

CARTER: But ...

WESTON: What?

CARTER: All this is a mystery.

WESTON: Happiness is hidden in this state.

CARTER: I don't agree with you.

WESTON: Whether you agree or not, death is eternal truth. Life is one hundred per cent false.

CARTER: Your ideas are skewered. This is why you despair.

WESTON: I'm quite right.

CARTER: There is no matter of right or wrong.

WESTON: You can't ignore anything which is fact.

CARTER: Only men who avoid it are happy.

WESTON: They also embrace death.

CARTER: Death is fact. All pass this way.

WESTON: All pass. But all forget. All try to ignore but everyone is caught in its powerful clutch.

CARTER: There must always be fruitful discussion.

WESTON: [*Long pause*] Listen. One day, your fruitfulness will become mockery. Your ideas will become hollow.

CARTER: [*Long pause*] Uncle, my findings are different.

WESTON: My findings are one hundred per cent true. It is my addiction that I always try to ascertain facts. I don't ignore that which is unpleasant. I regard both well and unwell.

CARTER: This is good, and I expect good in everyone. I follow this path and am very happy. I recommend others do the same.

WESTON: One day, all your dreams will be shattered and you will see reality – you will begin to say that the world is futile – the world is godless – the world is full of thorns – the world is a cheat – and life is absurd.

CARTER: Let the time come. I'll see all this. Virtues terminate all woes and sorrows. Our forefathers told us and I follow them.

WESTON: Virtues are all meaningless in this world. Once death embraces us all, virtues sink as the sun sets.

CARTER: Forget death and learn to live happily.

WESTON: Forgetting the most powerful agency of the world is not a solution. It is just like closing your eyes to save you from the deep.

CARTER: [*Long pause*] Let all this happen. Come to think about your happy life. I know its way.

WESTON: You know nothing. Death is the most powerful agency monitoring all of us.

CARTER: No.

Lights down.

Act 2

Lights up.

CARTER brings two cups of coffee – one for WESTON and another for himself.

WESTON:	[*Long pause*] Perhaps you are on honeymoon?
CARTER:	[*Long pause. Smiles*] Yes!
WESTON:	Now you are in the realm of bodily bliss which is momentary.
CARTER:	It is not an issue.
WESTON:	No, this is only one matter.
CARTER:	How?
WESTON:	[*Smilingly*] Now everything seems as beautiful as roses. Even the desert will seem a forest.
CARTER:	How?
WESTON:	Now you can't know.
CARTER:	Why?
WESTON:	[*Smilingly*] During the honeymoon the sun seems millimetres away.
CARTER:	No.
WESTON:	I'm quite right. Believe me.
CARTER:	[*Feels shame*] You are mocking me.
WESTON:	You will know.
CARTER:	When?
WESTON:	When the time comes.
CARTER:	Okay, uncle. Please ...!
WESTON:	[*Long pause*] Today I have seen your wife in a very pleasant mood. Never before!

CARTER: When?

WESTON: When she was entering the cabin.

CARTER: Okay, uncle. Bless us for our happy conjugal life.

WESTON: My hearty blessings and best wishes!

CARTER: Thanks, uncle!

WESTON: She seems very smart. She seems cute.

CARTER: But for me she is much more.

WESTON: I understand your feelings. She is your wife, so she is definitely much more than anyone or anything in the world.

CARTER: [*Shows her photograph*] She is my bliss.

WESTON: You are right. It also happened to me during my honeymoon. But over time, all my dreams were shattered. Now I see her simply as my wife. I have forgotten the hot words I used to address her with. She has also forgotten such words. Now we always think about our life.

CARTER: [*Pause*] Uncle, you seem a very romantic person.

WESTON: [*Laughs*] Ha ... ha!

CARTER: Please excuse me.

WESTON: Say.

CARTER: [*Laughingly*] Give me a few words from your honey-moon dictionary.

WESTON: [*Laughs*] Ha ... ha!

CARTER: [*Laughs*] Ha ... ha!

WESTON: [*Smilingly*] You fill my heart with recollections of past dreams.

CARTER: Aha! Aha! Uncle! People say.

WESTON: [*Smilingly*] How beautiful you look! How much you love me! I will bring you the moon and sun within a moment if you ask. There is no one prettier than you in the whole world. You are far better-greater-prettier than the peerless beauty, Helen. I don't like to go anywhere without you even for a moment. I will die for you and you will be in my arms when I depart for the heavenly seat under the Tree.

CARTER: Now?

WESTON: Thoughts of the past. Never to occur in the future. Just like a mirage.

CARTER: How romantic you are, uncle!

WESTON: [*Laughs*] Ha ... ha!

CARTER: Really, very romantic.

WESTON: I can't say.

CARTER: You are a very romantic person. So, you should avoid feelings of isolation, alienation, fear, insecurity and loneliness.

WESTON: I avoid it but it all occurs naturally.

CARTER: Sometimes, the sense of despair embraces anyone.

WESTON: It is not embraced, rather inherited.

CARTER: [*Long pause*] Uncle, do you sing? Uncle, please ...!

WESTON: I can sing but you won't like it.

CARTER: Why?

WESTON: Because it tells bitter truths.

CARTER: Okay. No matter. Sing.

WESTON: [*Sings a lyric melancholically*]

Man does every right and wrong to bargain –
Childhood in the lap of sire and mom's born –
In young age hoping to gain pleasure.
But it sinks in the evening treasure –
Leaving all memories as thorns in life –
Calling unexpected old age with knife –
Without any mercy, pleasure and love
For the naked cold deep bed in the grave.

CARTER: Oh! Oh! Too much elegiac! Each pitch and stress is bloody and elegiac.

WESTON: But it touches the truth.

CARTER: [*Long pause*] Oh! This is the world? This is the life?

WESTON: [*Long pause*] Please excuse me.

CARTER: Ask me.

WESTON: May I ask you something?

CARTER: Okay.

WESTON: Does your wife love you?

CARTER: Yes.

WESTON: How much?

CARTER: [*Surprised. Laughs*] Ha … ha! Very much!

WESTON: How much?

CARTER: It's a meaningless question.

WESTON: Sorry. Please understand. I would like to know its value and quantity.

CARTER: She loves me enough.

WESTON: What is its quantity?

CARTER: [*Laughs*] You can understand.

WESTON: I know the meaning of love of the honeymoon days.

CARTER: What?

WESTON: Do you like to know?

CARTER: If you know, tell me.

WESTON: Its value is till you develop a daily routine.

CARTER: What is new in it?

WESTON: Know it. Its value is to recall it and repent one's whole life for such deeds. Finally, all things of value from the honeymoon days sink fully.

CARTER: Such happiness sinks which is under the compass of time, place and mortalities. Our love is beyond all this. Our love shines as a polar star in the sky. We know its formula.

WESTON: You don't know the world and its people.

CARTER: None knows the whole world.

WESTON: You are quite right. But ...!

CARTER: I know not all well but know well enough to live happily.

WESTON: You miss something. You fail to understand the exact position of the world and its harsh realities.

CARTER: What?

WESTON: The world is not in your fist.

CARTER: I do understand all this.

WESTON: The world will cheat you. People will cheat you – specially, who is your favourite? Beware of your favourites!

CARTER: My wife is my favourite and I share my all with her. She is my life – she is my breath. I live for her and she lives for me. We will die together. We have made such promises and we will fulfil them.

WESTON: You live in a world of emotions which is more dangerous than any other physical thing in the world.

CARTER: No.

WESTON: You are wrong.

CARTER: You are wrong.

WESTON: Time will tell.

CARTER: It will answer according to my deeds.

WESTON: It is not certain.

CARTER: Right, but we all live in expectation.

WESTON: We all live in the realm of expectation and it is never fulfilled. One after another ... it changes one by one. No limit of expectations and finally, we leave this false world making our life absurd.

CARTER: Saints and philosophers also say the world is false. But they don't know the real pleasure which we enjoy in our conjugal life.

WESTON:	So, I say life is absurd.
CARTER:	We are not saints ... we are not philosophers.
WESTON:	It is fact that life is absurd. The whole world is absurd for man. It is for all beings except man.
CARTER:	Life is absurd for those who suffer lifelong and are unable to provide even a square meal.
WESTON:	The people who don't suffer also meet the same as those who do suffer, even for food and clothing. They are buried in the same graves. Their bodies are changed into the same elements after death. They also enter the eternal chaos quite unknown by others in the world.
CARTER:	None needs know it.
WESTON:	But they have keen interest knowing it.
CARTER:	Yes. But this is the mystery. This is the reason why the world continues.
WESTON:	This is the reason man lives in illusion and the darkness of ignorance.
CARTER:	This is only known by the supreme agency of God.
WESTON:	There is no God.
CARTER:	God is our supreme commander. God is our supreme power.
WESTON:	[*Exclamatory*] No ... no! There is no God.
CARTER:	Who is our supreme power?
WESTON:	Nature.
CARTER:	Nature?
WESTON:	Yes.
CARTER:	Is Nature above God?
WESTON:	Nature is above all. There is no God.
CARTER:	Are you a pagan?
WESTON:	No!
CARTER:	No?

WESTON:	No!
CARTER:	You must know this. The world will melt without God within a moment. God is the Supreme Power who commands each and everything in the world – each and every activity of the world?
WESTON:	We all are commanded by the cycle of Nature. The cycle of night and day – the cycle of life and death – the cycle of loss and gain – the cycle of joys and sorrows.
CARTER:	But be sure, uncle! God is beyond all – God is above all.
WESTON:	What has been got by you from God?
CARTER:	Everything.
WESTON:	Whatever you have got will be lost and you will go from here leaving every thing. Not even a jot will be taken by you for your future home – in the same way you brought nothing with you from your previous life. No?
CARTER:	But I am happy here.
WESTON:	Think properly. You see man becoming pale, weeping and dying and going from here. None remembers him after death. Nothing in this world can give fire to his body. Nothing in this world can award breath to one who is in the grave. No hymn can awaken him from the grave. Know it!
CARTER:	Right, but there is no meaning of all this in life.
WESTON:	Why?
CARTER:	The things which are beyond our reach should be ignored.
WESTON:	But facts should be dealt with.
CARTER:	It is meaningless. Generations have passed but no answer discovered. The earth is the same and man continues to come and go.
WESTON:	All went meaninglessly. Though they thought the same as we think.
CARTER:	Right. But except all this, none has an option.

WESTON:	This is the reason that we live in the darkness of ignorance and in the state of expectations which are never fulfilled and finally, we depart from here for an unknown place which is quite dark.
CARTER:	Really, quite unknown, but not a matter of despair.
WESTON:	We don't gain it, rather it is natural. It embraces us automatically. It welcomes us naturally, though we persistently try to ignore and stay away from its powerful agency.
CARTER:	We do whatever is necessary for us.
WESTON:	Most people ignore this fact and you do the same.
CARTER:	I do what is presently necessary as all others do.
WESTON:	Whatever everyone does ends in loss and the embracing of death.
CARTER:	But we have to do whatever may be its outcome.
WESTON:	I also do and know that the world is barren.
CARTER:	The world is not barren, rather we enjoy and later we return to our home for renewal. It is also important for us. Death renews us.
WESTON:	Whether it renews us or not, it is quite dark. We don't know its meaning and our primary home. Our past is unknown. Our present is also unknown. Our future is unknown. We are here as irremediable exiles. We live in the home of others.
CARTER:	No.
WESTON:	Why?
CARTER:	We all live in our own home.
WESTON:	Quite wrong.
CARTER:	Why? We have our own existence. Man is the most perfect being in the cosmos.
WESTON:	None is perfect in this universe. There is no existence of God. Life is absurd. Although other beings exist, their life is meaningful. This world is their home.

CARTER: The cosmos without man is meaningless.

WESTON: This hollow world needs not man. Man is hollow.
            Society is hollow. All our institutions are hollow. They
            only take us to the edge of loss. They take us to death.

CARTER: This is society which provides maximum facilities and
            takes nothing of goodness.

WESTON: This hollow institution can do nothing for mankind.

CARTER: This is the only agency which cares for us without fees.

WESTON: You don't know this.

CARTER: I know and enjoy.

WESTON: In this state of knowledge and enjoyment all are taken
            to absurdity.

CARTER: There is no option. So, we must ignore it all.

WESTON: The hollowness of the world swallows us all and we
            reach home that is quite alien. We can see all this in
            your family.

CARTER: They all are fine. We all are fine.

WESTON: Know, you will meet the same which has been met by
            your forefathers.

CARTER: But ...

WESTON: One day, your own will carry your body to the
            graveyard mercilessly. No tears will be produced by
            them. Your own will take you to the crematorium. Your
            body will be burnt as wood for fuel.

CARTER: Naturally.

WESTON: Naturally, life is absurd. You will also embrace death.
            Your wife whom you love and who loves you will
            become meaningless. She will not go with you to the
            grave though she says she loves you and you love her.

CARTER: No. She really loves me.

WESTON: Believe! Only floral tributes will be paid. Only rituals for
            their sake will be fulfilled. But nothing in the world will
            then be meaningful for you.

CARTER: I'm a manager of a great company and my income is large. If I fall ill, all will take me to hospital.

WESTON: They will take, but when death occurs all will take you to the crematorium or graveyard.

CARTER: My family is very civilised and they will do whatever is possible.

WESTON: Whatsoever, but absurd. You must know it!

CARTER: All are highly educated. Most have doctorates. I also possess a doctoral degree. My wife is just my double.

WESTON: All is absurd.

CARTER: It is the degree which enables me to be recognised as a great man in society.

WESTON: This recognition will be mocked in time. Just wait.

CARTER: No.

WESTON: When death occurs, your affinity and degrees go in vain.

CARTER: No.

WESTON: Realise this, it's one hundred per cent true.

CARTER: Yes, I realise that but I have to continue the journey of life like others. So, such reasons are stupid.

WESTON: No. It is fact and we must accept the fact that life is absurd.

CARTER: But ...

WESTON: Happily or unhappily, we all reach the same place.

CARTER: [*Long pause*] My wife is my only hope and I share all my feelings and emotions with her.

WESTON: You don't. She does the same.

CARTER: How does man live here? Why does man live here?

WESTON: The world is hollow. The cosmos is hollow. There are thorns all around us.

CARTER: But ...

WESTON: All is meaningless.

CARTER: Has this world no love?

WESTON: There is no love in the universe. No joy in this world.

CARTER: No love?

WESTON: Nothing in the name of love!

CARTER: God! But God commands us.

WESTON: Believe me, there is no God.

CARTER: But all believe.

WESTON: God is a myth.

CARTER: That is an insult to the Supreme Power.

WESTON: There is no power in God's name.

CARTER: His reign is beyond question.

WESTON: There is no such a reign in its name.

CARTER: I'm unable to question His reign.

WESTON: Has anyone seen God?

CARTER: People say.

WESTON: All say – all believe – but all this myth is transferred from generation to generation – and is meaningless too!

CARTER: All live in this state.

WESTON: You are right. It has been inherited by all of us in this isolated place till we reach our home.

CARTER: Is this not our home?

WESTON: No.

CARTER: Oh! This is not our home?

WESTON: No. We have not our home and our home is unseen. So, our life is absurd. Life is false. Death is true. After it, whether there is existence of our soul or not is quite unknown.

CARTER: I've had different experiences. My relatives are also very fortunate and happy with life. I've also got a very good life partner.

WESTON: She is false. All are false. She will cheat you. Women are more than other things in the world. They are just like falling stars. You don't know the world.

CARTER: I've a friend who is just like me and always cooperates with me – always cooperates with us. Whenever we are in need he serves us as a servant.

WESTON: Friendship is meaningless.

CARTER: No.

WESTON: You are wrong.

CARTER: There is no man without friend.

WESTON: There is no friend of anyone. Believe.

CARTER: [Long pause] We also cooperate with him when in need.

WESTON: This is the weakness which will swallow you all. There is no friend of anyone in the world. We all are alone. The concept of friendship is false.

CARTER: Why do you say all this?

WESTON: I know.

CARTER: Nothing in this name?

WESTON: Nothing ... nothing. Friend is an illusion, like a mirage.

CARTER: We always pine for friends – we welcome friends – we expect the whole world to be our friend.

WESTON: This is a mirage. There is no friend.

CARTER: How can you justify your position?

WESTON: See the world – see the people dying and weeping – see the people in woe and trouble. Where are the friends to wipe away their tears? Is there anyone to die with them or to suffer with them? None shares in woes and sorrows. All share in joys and property. The world is false. Man lives with expectations which are never fulfilled. Life is absolutely meaningless.

CARTER: [Long pause] Oh! World! People!

WESTON: Friend is a delusion – it is an illusion just like bubbles.

CARTER:	The world is not as you say. If yes, how do people live here?
WESTON:	Man is helpless to live here in this very situation. Except he has no option.
CARTER:	You say all this because of the degeneration of your body's organs. I am young and my approach is different. I am happy with life.
WESTON:	I'm also happy with life, because I have no other option. I'm to live in the same state whether I like it or not. You are muttering some lyrical lines. Can you sing them?
CARTER:	Yes.
WESTON:	Sing.
CARTER:	[*Sings a lyric in joy*]

Heavenly pleasure in the lap of queen
As in the full moon night for the dawn.
Past, present and future are not away –
All in my fist by God's mercy, all okay.
Life is blissful and fairies all around –
A lyric written in heavenly sound.
Future in the shade of sages in heaven
Where everyone is quite well and even.

WESTON:	Your lyrics are as hollow as an oak tree. Quite a lie!
CARTER:	No.
WESTON:	You are a child.
CARTER:	Uncle, this is the main reason for your despair.
WESTON:	But I do not agree with you.

Lights down.

ACT 3

Lights up.

HELENA arrives and begins to talk to her husband, CARTER.

HELENA   [*Very calmly and gently*] Will you take me to the cinema hall?

CARTER: Yes.

HELENA: When?

CARTER: At noon.

HELENA: Okay.

            [*Long pause*]

CARTER: Why are you sad now?

HELENA: I am not sad.

CARTER: If you say. Sit here.

HELENA: [*Sits*] Why are you passing time here? I was alone in the cabin, waiting for you. How can I live alone there?

CARTER: I'm so sorry. Fortunately, today I met an uncle who is sitting with us and began talking to him. I understand your feelings, Helena.

HELENA: [*Towards Weston*] My pleasure.

CARTER: [*Gets a cup of coffee*] Have a cup of coffee.

HELENA: Thanks, Carter.

CARTER: [*Gives a cup of coffee*] Take it Uncle.

WESTON: Thanks, Carter.

CARTER: It will refresh us.

            [*Pause*]

WESTON: [*Calmly and gently. Indicating to HELENA*] Perhaps ... your wife?

CARTER: Yes.

WESTON: She is very gentle and pretty. I bless you and wish you a happy conjugal life.

CARTER: Thanks, uncle.

HELENA: Thanks, uncle.

WESTON: My pleasure. A very fine couple! Nature has rewarded you.

CARTER: He is a very gentle man, Helena.

HELENA: Of course.

ROBERT arrives. There is a badge pinned to his shirt on which his name is written.

ROBERT: What are you doing here, Helena?

HELENA: [Silent]

ROBERT: Helena?

HELENA: [Silent]

ROBERT: With whom you have come here?

HELENA: [Looks at CARTER. Silent]

ROBERT: With Carter?

HELENA: Yes?

ROBERT: Why?

CARTER: Who's this man, Helena?

HELENA: I don't know.

ROBERT: She's my wife.

CARTER: She's my wife! She is my life!

WESTON: Now she seems a thorn and not your wife.

ROBERT: She is my wife. I've been searching for her for the past three days but couldn't find her. She's cheated me. She has broken all the promises she made to me.

CARTER: She's my wife. I have married her and we have promised to live together. None can snatch her. She's mine, not yours.

~ 38~

ROBERT: She is mine.

CARTER: She is mine ... mine ... mine.

WESTON: Oh! What is the matter?

CARTER: Uncle, you can say what is right and what is wrong?

WESTON: Yes, I have seen you with her for the past three days. It seems she is really your wife.

CARTER: You are quite right, uncle.

WESTON: Do you know him, Helena?

HELENA: No.

WESTON: Why do you not scold him? Why do you not say to him to go away from here?

CARTER: Right, uncle!

HELENA: Carter will say.

CARTER: [*Angrily*] ROBERT, go away from here now, otherwise you'll be sorry!

ROBERT: I will see you.

CARTER: We are three. You are alone.

ROBERT: You are also alone.

CARTER: Please help me, uncle.

WESTON: This is a personal matter.

CARTER: Can't?

WESTON: How? This is a matter of women. I can't interfere with any woman. No one can catch a falling star. I suggest you solve it yourselves.

CARTER: [*Angrily*] Helena, tell him flatly to leave, otherwise I will call the police. He is a devil. He is behind us.

HELENA: You should say. It is the duty of one's husband.

CARTER: Okay. Come and help me. I will fight him.

HELENA: I can't. I don't feel well, I told you last night. I am too tired.

CARTER: Okay. I will fight him on my own.

HELENA: But I do not like fighting.

CARTER: Why?

HELENA: Violence is not good for mankind.

CARTER: But man has to fight to exist.

ROBERT: You can't hold my wife. Helena is mine.

CARTER: She is mine. She is my dream and for her I will sacrifice my all.

            [*Takes a very big knife from his pocket and holds it in his hand*]

ROBERT: [*Takes a knife from his pocket. Runs towards CARTER. Attacks him*] Come and fight.

CARTER: [*Holding a big and edgy knife. Attacks him*] Come and fight.

ROBERT: [*Sighs. Falls on the ground, wounded and covered with blood. Dying*] Oh! My God! Oh my God! Oh my God. You have snatched my woes and sorrows. Thanks Carter.

CARTER: [*Sighs. Falls on the ground, wounded and covered with blood. Dying*] Oh my God! Oh my God. Oh! Oh! I'm dying. Let me die. Thank God. Thanks Robert.

WESTON: Oh! Oh! Oh God! Oh God! Let them fight. Let them die.

CARTER: [*Pleading*] Can you ... uncle?

WESTON: Oh! Oh! O my God! O my God! [*Leaves*]

CARTER: [*CARTER talking to HELENA*] Can you, darling Helena?

HELENA: I wish you a happy return to your home! [*Leaves*]

CARTER: [*Sarcastically*] Heartily thanks uncle! Thanks Helena. Thanks for leaving me alone.

A melancholic lyric entitled 'Life is a short time ...' is heard from an unknown direction. Tears are falling from the eyes of the people present and sitting on other nearby benches.

> Life is a short time bubble to disappear
> Before eyes leaving man never to cheer.
> Man is alien and homeless with furies –

Who departs from here without memories.
Life is a mirage that fully chews man.
Life is a palace made of minute sands
And shades where everyone dwells
During irremediable exile
And disappears by the time's missile.

Lights down.